Synapse Flies into Startle

The Orgasm Book

Sally Naylor

A Publication of The Poetry Box®

Editing & Book Design by Shawn Aveningo Sanders
Cover Art is derived from an original painting by Sally Naylor
Cover Layout & Design by Shawn Aveningo Sanders

ISBN: 978-1-948461-79-5
Printed in the United States of America.
Wholesale Distribution via Ingram.

Published by The Poetry Box®, 2021
Portland, Oregon
ThePoetryBox.com

The orgasm has replaced the cross as the focus of longing and the image of fulfillment.

—Malcolm Muggeridge

(The simple instant of perfect hunger—Yes)
how beautifully swims
the fooling world in my huge blood,
cracking brains   A swiftlyenormous light
—and furiously puzzling through, prismatic, whims
the chattering self perceives with hysterical fright

a comic tadpole wriggling in delicious mud

—e e cummings

Contents

~|~

Orgasm, silk
or the crawling into your own beast's belly?
Pinnacle? An arc? Enigma? Parachute?
Astonishment or query?

Urge

Drunk on ink joy, I'm sculpting consonants into rapture, considering
my obsessions. Is orgasm as close to God as I'll ever come or is it
metaphor? Disease? Why do the lowly & the holy so often intrigue?

Why zig-zag my smart-ass libido in loop de loops across white landscape
probing essence of orgasm? Fear of death or intimate atrocities?

Is it the O, O of self, selflessly offering up an Elysium paradox, poet's prayer
or mere landgrab? Is it time for adverbs to parse & fuck grammatically?

To witness & to merge: to share skin, worship invention. Now. Light
as the serious clowns of our collaborative, wet, pulsing concoctions.

I seek the gate into the garden, seek to become mere
seed, take root, leaf up, then become misting, earth-bound

flesh-scents, to bud, to sprout, to knead, to stroke, to mouth.
O to feather, tingle, then harden & fly all synapse into startle.

No time clocks in, only the coupling, the need to morph into an other,
an ether, as voices fizzle into infinite threads of unchurched tensions.

Space of trinity, of twins: our you, our me, all the god-self darlings made flesh.
Fallen yet holy, the *adagio to presto* of Arcangelo Corelli. Semen. Amen. Amen.

Holy Ontology, Batman

Distracting myself at nineteen from being nineteen, I read Sartre's
Being & Nothingness, Camus, Heidegger & several slate-grey, Russian winters.
Trying to care whether existence precedes essence. Trying. To care.

As ennui dons a black beret, I tire of monotony. No more *Crime & Punishment*
or *Anna Karenina*. Farewell, pathos of artistic suffering.
Adieu to *Emma Bovary's* nihilism & the fraternal order of the idiots Karamazov.

Shedding pseudo-smart, I leapfrog, hop-skip & June bug jump-it,
over coming of age markers—avoiding the academy's effete designer hell
as well as redemptive woo-woo mantras.
I hug Whitman's scraggly grey beard & high, unabashed vigor
for *A leaf of grass is no less than the journeywork of the stars.*

Bold & erudite enough, eventually,
to be fuck-you fluent in both ease & light,
I'll not get back to you with answers, unlike Sartre,
passe before he dies, who never knows
how to furnish a home orgasm by orgasm
or that *to be with those I love is enough.*

The Sex of Language

Earth laughs in flowers
—Emerson

Copulation—as clinical as an antiseptic mouth swab,
wears sensible shoes & a white lab coat of polyester;

it declaims its palaver in expository, polysyllabic,
peer-reviewed, well-documented, Latinate-based prose.

But consider the yellow powder, stem, pistil, stamen, roots
the seductions of ruffled leaf, of fluted vessel,
of quiver & entwine, of the seminal flowering
into the unfurling blossoms of the Lady Slipper or Blue Danube Orchid,
of lush rainforest, rife with moisture—

consider the contagions and persuasions of formal literary propagations—
compare that to the more idiomatic: screw, fuck—the happy gyrations
of my opening remarks & sallies, riding the salty thrusts of your body
through to epilogue.

Lovers I Have Had & Been

Duped early on by sham swains selling "gimme, gimme" games,
too many orgasms faked as faux beaux, no shows & early lovers-in-chief
salute my cock tease, while that penultimate chorus line
of *to have & to hold* gigolos struts its stuff.

Morphing later into a smoldering, wordsmith in heat, lover on top, Shh.
Close your eyes, going down now, back bent,
become a serious sperm farmer singing riffs of *Ride, Sally, Ride*.

Legs spread or down on my knees, coquette for whom the whole wild sky longs.
Ecstasy & apogee, numinous wildflower & skylark, mirror & birth mother lover,
all wafer & wine. (Amen) A cannibalize your god flirt,
a myth-buster & kaon mistress. Yes, I no, it's not a contest.

Then slowly that needy, too-much lover:
a misplaced loyalty glutton, herself forgotten for love
of another other, gutted, all break-down, Purple Heart,
a fuck-you lover, desire swallowing the whole world,
that break-out, last damn fool lover, wondering
if she'll ever make it out of this book,

like bold swimmers in seminal broth seek safe harbor.
No more star-crossed, out-to-lunch, narcissistic (half-assed) rakes.
So, Mr. God-damn Cosmos, send another or recycle
that funny, kind, savvy, straight-arrow, lion-heart lover.

Send scores of unbanked orgasms at sunrise, breeze-crowned lovers,
lovers of pearl, of how it never ends, savor all the tumble down,
clover & honied lovers I have ever had or been.
So many buoyant (thank you) damn fine lovers. Rewind all sweet scents
& scream-out-loud, hill-top yowls, bring on the last hurrahs,
enthralled & all agog: O lazy-eyed girl: consummate earth & language lover,

dazzled in the going down. Deliver again one last flip, big top stud:
a Casanova *fini*, salted in biting irony: a-sizzle & pulsed
with expanding heart & cock. Such fine dervish lovers:
twirling, *pulled from one fire—pushed into another.*

After the Last Orgasm

oscillates

it becomes the (undulating) spiral
down
of a leaf or giggle,
            word fluff, half-oms   & slow-motion
sloppy scampers,

light breeze, soft bangles,

throbs pulsed round some bemused cleric's
imaginary homilies, harpsichord or string quartet sounds.
So many green whistles. So many high riddles.

As the last turn-all-dogma-sideways song   crescendos,
in a final, up-side down broadcast
from the control tower, iterating,
then, reiterating, what it already knows:

Ceiling and visibility unlimited.

Transformed into playgrounds peopled with John Cleese silly walks,
a puppy's zig-zag wobble or crown of sonnets, while you loll about, Ms. O,
wondering if the future hinges
                more   on your deft fingers or his midnight tongue?

Poet on the Half-Shell: *Crazy Salad*

If I could just let go of Jung's dream of holocaust on a train & I can, then I'd walk right out of Poet's House, up Chambers Street to the A line—in a light rain with a backpack full of Battery Park lyrics, in the spring, insouciant, in full sunlight, indecipherable: inciting action, rising action, orgasm, falling, denouement, you know the score. Dropping all the maybes. *Fini.* Discarding scripts, I chant *Blessed, Blessed*, sweeter than haiku, Wordsworth, hibiscus or my work ethic. Yes, no more sharp elbows, just a marriage of Matisse, baby toes or plyers. No more black & whites. Get woke. Disengage. Let go. Ignore crossfire. Walk off page, leave stage. Launch *coup d'état*, light candles, for God is no fugue, prose poem, no stained-glass story or cathedral. Only glory, in the air, in awe, for *God is a verb & so am I.* Inciting action. O wonders inexhaustible. Enlightened. Transcendental, such grace, at ease as my voice stops trying to name me. In this budding spring, this temple, in the now & now gone, more plum than prune. Yes, romantic, even conventional, kind of cheesy. Bounced like some vagabond's fantasy – this urge to pass through & never to own, *in media res*. In love. Sexed. Buzzed electric. Salty. Undefined yet explicit. Rogue, free & holy skeptic. Yes, one hot mess. Spun halfway to Venus – such an orgasm tumbled—its thick iambic brogue falls from my tongue, honied, immaculate in astonished frenzies—shot beyond all meaning in its arc, airs, aria & elegy.

For the Seekers

What I want to know is how to kiss
those social scientists goodbye:
so specific, measurable, concrete,
hugging stats, graphs, case histories,
smelling a lot like goals in lab coats.

How to say yes to the great lie, the hope that after engorgement
or any other promising venue, after all the undulations:
the symphony, improv, sonnet or drama of orgasm
how to still believe the myth that you will be released from self,

if only for moments

from the longing to be one, to be separate
from all that longing
for where in the wanting of release
is release?

Which you will learn and learn again
and as always, you don't
won't get there or anywhere.

Pilgrim, tell me how to sabotage, integrate or embrace the great lies?
Is there a hint in the communion of joining and getting nowhere
together or is that just more mirage? What I really want to know is . . .

~||~

What is orgasm?
A final respite from the fretful itch;
last ticket to invincible gatherings;
an ease of burgeoning labial tremors;
semicolons
extending a promise of connection?

A Fabulous Tower, Long Rapunzel Hair & Yes

this tiny ballerina is no accounts receivable.
Head bowed, hand over heart, hands clasped in prayer,
we know her to be a devout, but only in the electric riff
or private temple of her dreams, as she chants *Red Rover, Red Rover.*

After the tomboy years, Miss O harpsichords a fevered
Brandenburg, clamors to reach out, fiddle, learn languages without ears,
retrieve her first cradle: breath like two golden fish, float, cut bait.

How she pirouettes beyond her Faberge Egg: nest and prison,
wanting to belong, to claim an address or body,
resign from all bogus love me, love me marathons,
to savor freedom: a concerto. O rhapsody. Plie. Leap. Sway.

Webster's Concise offers no glimmer or knowing in its cognition,
lacks negative capability. Twirl, girl, as your fairy tale cursive
undulates with rain, death, the lotus, high notes & hunger,
fresh from what happens (O, O, O) to haiku in a tutu, rain or the soul.

From the Red Couch of How We Cherish

Turning on our sides, we settle, nestling
into the twin spoons of an old urge,

our arms wrapped tightly, you cocoon
me as we meet in that final field—

cradled from behind by your thighs
arms enveloping my torso, you tucked neatly

behind me as I burrow my bottom into your lap,
where amidst the impulse of your fleshy rococo

our bodies slow into mere bone facts,
and skin disperses an ease beyond

language, sky or burgeoning –
until waves collapse. It is like this.

Morphed particles of a quantum something,

let's call it arc or the half-life of a breeze
jujitsu in repose, maybe, or numinous.

Slip into it. Nuzzle the sweet mortal impetus
of all holdings. Now. Hold on. Breathe. That.

Quirky Jukebox Song

We know some things about things, but not what to expect,

like how to harvest mythical wings from extravagant clouds
or on Tuesdays, how to breathe or toast the shining bubbles

of bounce-back stanzas, with a yes to the lilt & resonance
of electric innards & a desire-to-worship twang,

or of the thrumming spitfire of fuel-injected vibes,
in search of laughter, journey, play. Immortality?

In search of home, body, mission, orgasms lined up only to out,
like the sonic apostles of fine crystal, a green grace or the slow shuffle

of a Boogie Woogie: step in, step out, turn yourself about,
like late afternoon fingers clutch the breeze as dandelion seeds

drift in wisps: updrafts, how airy batches of elegant fragments,
hint at Salvador Dali or a *Deus Ex Machina* moment—

we look next for the pole-vault of our rescue gods, that chorus
of jazzy crescendos in a wonky, get-down, jukebox Halleluiah.

Pitching Woo

Love is not the body, but it is of the body.

Let this remain the sun in preamble,
the last murmur before release.
For ours is the dance greened with buds –
part cilantro, part surf. Breathe.

In Chagall's *Birthday*,

we levitate
as you hover, slightly above,
bouquet in hand,
neck craned backwards.

Somewhere beyond the mirth of your O, so radiant face
sing a chorus of fern tendrils, laced with fervor & nutmeg.

Pan-piping flutes laud your wily goat's grace
as sea gulls spiral the landscape

while slow-motion pirouettes float us higher higher.

For it is summer in paradise & we are eons away from our old lives or gravity.

Already

we've started in
with the lovey, dovey,
smoochie, kissy face,
the full moon spooning,
the panting,
and already it's too late;
it's always been too late
to stop.
We live for the universe of touch,
and how it plays out this time and the next and the next
how it never cloys
how we are maestros
to the gods, how we transcend
how blessed we are to have such skin
electric, galvanized, kinetic.
Come my beautiful cock, let's sin.

time tender fun

my gift is not this poem but the space around it

the white ethers

in which push dissipates
as grip erases its fist
& history its elbow rights
to the future

here lies the ivory canopy in all its arc & graceful span
soft as care or quiet after orgasm

an ease as open as an Egret's strut
neck forward, atop that surge

some merger of intimacies
it is a peace vast as weather or river or medley

as we tap dance stretch improvise sky

dive maybe savor

because it's time tender fun & because we can

valentine

~III~

Orgasm?

What grief sounds like
when joy calls in the dark.

Mere salt or hunger?
Cathedrals or a story?

As yes cradles its yes,
the benediction
of an infinite sonata trilling.

Curriculum Vitae

Fueled by an impetus beyond catechism or grammar,
this wordsmith prefers the fray to communion.

Despite meditation & Earl Grey tea
a brass-knuckled revolutionary,
active in rearrangement, persnickety in syntax,
she tosses the confetti of an animated diction
& peppers it with a school-girl dereliction.

Delirious with late afternoon hibiscus & bevies of Great Blue Herons,
her idealism wears small black patent leather shoes & the waistcoat
of a polysyllabic, Latinate-based, Percy Bysshe Shelly
spouting dubious aphorisms.

Nurtured on Queen Anne's Lace, too
often, she stops breathing—like Emily
goes it alone, living *zero at the bone*.
Can you or anyone keep her
from the terrible schism & what about
                the knotting & twisting beneath

her jaunty *Hail to thee blithe spirit* patina?

So tell me, please do, Mr. God-damned Cosmos,
just who will now save or hire this skylark poet?
Orgasm or you?

Somehow

we have got beyond our aversion to the rote,
and even the hungers of more and more,
we have spiraled sideways into our little dreaming room.

And what a relief
to have those other years
behind. All that duty-walking through decades,
with just enough to keep going,
to keep push-pulling, inching ever so slightly towards myself, and then
delightful,

finally, the long puzzle of you.

So now, upside down we float   towards each other
intersecting somewhere above splendor
                                                            or Monet's water lilies
beyond   all throb and reverberation, our necks craned, whimsical,
                  adrift like some painting of clouds painting clouds

or that's the story I tell myself: you, me, all startle and coupling,
psalms composed in skin time. Fingertips, tongues, teeth. Breathe.

To Couple

I always wanted to live in music,
maybe Pachelbel, Corelli or one of the Brandenburg's
loving the covenant, the dazzle,
the pure, bold Mozart sun of it,
become all April
scudding clouds,
rain
showers, haiku,
narcissus and violin prayers—

melody, counterpoint, crescendo,
like the body of a bird
stepping into God.

That kind of reach or surge. Join me.

Compelled

like the heat of young animals, harbinger of light
turned magnet to the other, needy, we drop

impatient into bed. How we string each other together,
all eyes, word play & funny bone, in fizzle & persiflage.

We'd do it alone, we'd do it for eons even if our mission
dissolved into ashes, sheer whimsey or the whistle

of deities, the verbal back flips, snide syllables, even
our trip wires & trampolines. Yes. We do it for love.

Yet we're not so lunatic or smug as to believe that
we were made for this, but

we were made for this.

Desire
gifts us a pulse that echoes forward,

& waits for us to catch up, then
whispers: *I will miss you when you're dead.*

Promissory Note

We make meaning & create stories with symbols, such poor little coffins,
for *this is the way the world ends*, next to the ink & memory of skin, laughter,
smooth dance moves, well-used linen or the clink of fine crystal.

Look to the concrete not abstractions, look to active verbs & the Anglo-Saxon.
Nouns. Statements not questions. For just where is the atlas for loss of intimacy?

Do I dare flow into a world uncontained by structure?
Has it always been this way? And why now do I own the courage to forage?

When you've misplaced your lover, just how to fill a book
with orgasm? And why create crucibles as we order crutches?

Stop talking woman.
Soon it will be bonfire & wild raspberry season in County Charlevoix.
Don't muzzle your life beneath the blah, blah, blahs of longing.

That too will be celebrated, even as the Phoenix shakes
her electric feathers as a last semaphore of ash comes due
sent by the lucid, wild, terrified, vulgar pragmatist that is you.

Thrum

Like some young antelope dancing across the face of the moon,
her eyes fill with thank you, thank you tears.

Friend to the bobolink, happy to have been here, there, nowhere
anywhere, from the Upper East Side to Bay of Fundy frolics.

Such wilderness, no museum of disappointment, no ebony draped window,
a feisty prima donna, this sawgrass fabulous diva sings a salty maritime,
like a tap dance or new pink dress, a shit-naive feeling saying yes.

A glossy third eye stuck on her forehead, she sallies forth to Poet's House,
tremulous in high syncopated verses,
all snake-hips & hiss: hyperbole's own gadfly.
She is full of prayers or is it language?   Find her a god, man or poem to climb.

Replete with gimp-footed leaps & face-plant kerfuffles, she just is.
Safe in the now & having been-ness of her life.
Laughed, shuddered & still shuddering,
one quirky mechanic, tuning the orgasmic   how her hymns buzz.

Salt

Word.
Cock.

The infinity tasks.

All the hillsides dappled still each spring
with poppy fields & bee's wings
outside Sausalito. Desire eating the world.

If there is a way in, through
or out (or the time) finally
to know or tell about, deny,
recite or scout out, trumpet or bury,

a way to parse the raven-winged offerings
of this carnie, horde the keys to this enigma,
this mill of uncertainty, this salsa life,

laundry, shroud, lark, cat with violin inside,
resuscitate the dying, shut-mouthed lover,
the orange cones in a village of trolls, it is

this poet & her salts.

Orgasm.

Stamen & pistil chanting
a soft lilac rhetoric
or mortality unbandaged?

The immaculate stream
winding home, pulsed & steady
or a voice rife with tongues?

The first violin unfetters
as finale
reverberates her screams

Praise for *Synapse Flies into Startle*

An honest, uninhibited, brave exploration of those intimate moments when we are most vulnerable, most powerful, most bestial, most human, most alone, most united, most selfish, most generous, most profane, most sacred...told with wit, deep insight, delightful quirkiness, and profound sensitivity. It speaks to our most mysterious and unexplored common denominator. A book to savor!

—Lynda Pinto Torres

This feverish collection of poems interweaves sexual gymnastics with the poet's verbal foreplay in such a way that we are tossed in dizzying intoxication from mattress to mattress of her poetic aspirations. Sally Naylor's poems offer expansive meanings of the wondrous miracle of orgasm through numerous imaginative "sallies," such as "sonic apostles of fine crystal," "high riddles," "green whistles," "trip wires & trampolines,"—to name just a few definitions you will not find in the dictionary. This is a book where the world of the body and the body of poetry merge. For example, Naylor reveals the method to her madness in the appropriately titled, *CURRICULUM VITAE*, where "she tosses the confetti of an animated diction/ & peppers it with a school-girl dereliction." In other pieces we find ourselves "electric, galvanized, kinetic," amidst the inventions of her language. Hyper-hyphenated teasers include "raven-winged offerings," "hill-top yowls" and "god-self darlings." The sheer seduction of these poems leaves us, in Rumi's words, "pulled from one fire—" and "pushed into another."

—Deborah DeNicola

Sally Naylor's *Synapse Flies into Startle:The Orgasm Book* is a rap, a hoot, a song; it's the Fourth of July of love-making in words for flesh and lust. One does not read these poems, one revels in them. Naylor's free-fall and ramped-up romp in the haymaking of sex, love, not-love, almost love, some love, lovers, losers, orgasm and faked orgasms, scintillates with rhythmic, gyrating lines, and images of hypnotic synaptic firings in the brain and groin. These poems are not for the faint of heart or bashful. Naylor's honesty is unnerving, without inhibitions, no stop signs. They'll set your hair, loins and heart on fire.

—Lenny DellaRocca

Sally Naylor's poetry has always been, in her own words, "polysyllabic," but her "zig-zag . . . smart-ass libido" does special "loop de loops" in this particular tour de force, exploring orgasms and the search for the mythical G-spot of poetry. It makes me want to close my blinds, hunker down, and well, you can imagine the rest. As Sally says, "Get woke." Read this book: you're not likely to ever forget it.

—Barbra Nightingale, author of *Alphalexia*

About the Author

A three-legged stool, Sally Naylor is poet, therapist & teacher, Sally, studied with Campbell McGrath in the FIU MFA program; she thrived in classes with Maxine Kumin, Gerald Stern, Ilya Kaminsky & Tony Hoagland. Sally is associate editor of *SOFLOPOJO*, teaches community workshops for the Palm Beach Poetry Festival, writes memoir as well as text and workbooks for neophytes & now offers Zoomshops for emerging poets.

Below is a cento from the manuscript by way of a concise introduction:

Bold, unrepentant, ready: a kind of ginger, myth buster & koan mistress,
rogue, free & holy skeptic, all snake hips & hiss, hyperbole's own gadfly,
one quirky mechanic tuning the orgasmic how her hymns buzz.

For more information about her classes visit her website at:

www.writer'scatapult.com

About The Poetry Box®

The Poetry Box® is a boutique publishing company in Portland, Oregon, who provides a platform for both established and emerging poets to share their words with the world through beautiful printed books and chapbooks.

Feel free to visit the online bookstore (thePoetryBox.com), where you'll find more titles including:

Psyche's Scroll by Karla Linn Merrifield

Moroccan Holiday by Lauren Tivey

Shoebox by Donovan Hufnagle

My Miscellaneous Muse by Ralph La Rosa

Just the Girls by Pamela R. Anderson-Bartholet

Between States of Matter by Sherry Rind

Building a Woman by Deborah Meltvedt

The Kingdom of Birds by Joan Colby

Off Coldwater Canyon by C.W. Emerson

Excoriation by Rebecca Smolen

What She Was Wearing by Shawn Aveningo Sanders

My Mother Never Died Before by Marcia B. Loughran

Sophia & Mister Walter Whitman by Penelope Scambly Schott

and more . . .

www.ingramcontent.com/pod-product-compliance
Ingram Content Group UK Ltd.
Pitfield, Milton Keynes, MK11 3LW, UK
UKHW020136250726
13967UKWH00002B/697